The Blue and the Gray

Quilt Patterns using Civil War Fabrics

Mary Etherington and Connie Tesene

Martingale
Create with Confidence

The Blue and the Gray:
Quilt Patterns using Civil War Fabrics
© 2013 by Mary Etherington and Connie Tesene

Martingale®
19021 120th Ave. NE, Ste. 102
Bothell, WA 98011-9511 USA
ShopMartingale.com

Printed in China
18 17 16 15 14 13   8 7 6 5 4 3 2

Library of Congress Cataloging-in-Publication Data
is available upon request.

ISBN: 978-1-60468-254-0

Mission Statement

Dedicated to providing quality products and service to inspire creativity.

Credits

President & CEO: Tom Wierzbicki

Editor in Chief: Mary V. Green

Design Director: Paula Schlosser

Managing Editor: Karen Costello Soltys

Acquisitions Editor: Karen M. Burns

Technical Editor: Ursula Reikes

Copy Editor: Tiffany Mottet

Production Manager: Regina Girard

Illustrator: Ann Marra

Cover & Text Designer: Regina Girard

Photographer: Brent Kane

Contents

Fabric clubs are a big part of any quilt shop's business and at Country Threads, we are no different. We design our clubs to create customer loyalty, stimulate creativity, and above all, to make that trip to the mailbox a much-anticipated joy.

This book was developed from such a club and includes the 18 quilts ("Polly's Pair" is actually *two* quilts!) that were designed especially for our customers. At Country Threads we called this club the Civil War Club. In truth it developed because we had a whole building *full* of reproduction Civil War–era fabric . . . and to use some of that fabric, we came up with this plan. Every other month, we'd send out a new pattern along with eight fat eighths of fabric. We also included a bit of news from the shop and farm.

This popular club is now in its fourth year and still going strong. We think one reason for its popularity is that the patterns are traditional pieced blocks. We find our inspiration in state-sponsored quilt publications featuring antique quilts, magazines, and quilt squares. Coming up with a quilt design that's historically correct is somewhat impossible, try as we might. We would speculate that most quilts sent with the soldiers to battle were probably made up of simple squares . . . quick and easy. Since we can't claim to be experts in the field, we just go with the fact that we love the fabrics and try to keep the appliqué to a minimum!

Another reason the club remains popular is that the reproduction fabrics are created in colors that work so well in our homes today. Vibrant reds, stately navy blues and browns, good-old gold, and basic black make up the color palette of many of our quilts. The patterns in the fabrics are usually very subtle and small, and this also adds to the timeless quality of reproduction quilts. Also note that the quilts are very scrappy. This is our favorite type of quilt to make and allows lots of creativity with color and design. Normally all colors can be used together, but here are some of our favorite combinations that always seem to work.

- Red, pumpkin, teal, and navy
- Black, green, gold, and cranberry
- Navy, light blue, gray, and barn red
- Chocolate brown and red
- Pink and brown

The quilts in this book are easy to make. Specific piecing and stitching techniques are included in the patterns. To help you, pressing arrows are also included to indicate the best direction to press the seam allowances. However, if you need clarification on any techniques, such as rotary cutting, sewing borders on a quilt, making a quilt sandwich, or binding a quilt, visit ShopMartingale.com/HowtoQuilt. You can download free, illustrated how-to information to help you with your project.

We thank Martingale for asking us to write this book. Their trust in us is gratifying. You can find us in Iowa where we'll be working in the garden, playing with the dogs, cleaning our houses, and, of course, sewing. If you are in the neighborhood, please stop by. We would love to see you.

~ Connie and Mary

Troops in Formation

The uniform peaks on these Delectable Mountain blocks give the impression of soldiers in formation, whether on the rolling hills of Pennsylvania and Virginia, or in more rugged terrain of North Carolina.

Quilt size: 26½" x 32½"
Finished block: 4" x 4"

Materials

Yardages are based on 42"-wide fabric.
⅛ yard *each* of 8 light prints for blocks and pieced border
⅔ yard of brown fabric for setting triangles, corner squares, inner border, and binding
½ yard *total* of assorted medium or dark prints in red, blue, black, gold, and rust for blocks and pieced border
⅛ yard *each* of 4 red prints for blocks
⅛ yard *each* of 4 blue prints for blocks
1 yard of fabric for backing
30" x 36" piece of batting

Cutting

Measurements include ¼"-wide seam allowances.
From the brown fabric, cut:
1 strip, 7" x 42"; cut into the following:
- 4 squares, 7" x 7"; cut squares into quarters diagonally to yield 16 side setting triangles. You will have 2 left over.
- 2 squares, 5½" x 5½"; cut squares in half diagonally to yield 4 corner setting triangles. These are oversized and will be trimmed later.
4 squares, 1½" x 1½"
4 strips, 1" x 42"
3 binding strips, 2¼" x 42"

From the assorted medium and dark prints, cut:
150 squares, 1⅞" x 1⅞"; cut squares in half diagonally to yield 300 triangles

From the red prints, cut:
8 squares, 3⅞" x 3⅞"; cut squares in half diagonally to yield 16 triangles

From the blue prints, cut:
8 squares, 3⅞" x 3⅞"; cut squares in half diagonally to yield 16 triangles

From the light prints, cut:
16 squares, 3⅞" x 3⅞"; cut squares in half diagonally to yield 32 triangles
150 squares, 1⅞" x 1⅞"; cut squares in half diagonally to yield 300 triangles
32 squares, 1½" x 1½"

Making the Delectable Mountain Blocks

1 Sew a light 1⅞" triangle to a dark 1⅞" triangle. Press the seam allowances toward the dark triangle. Make six.

Make 6.

2 Sew a light 3⅞" triangle to a red or blue 3⅞" triangle. Press the seam allowances toward the red or blue triangle. Make one.

Make 1.

3 Join a light 1½" square, the six units from step 1, and the unit from step 2. Press the seam allowances as indicated. The block should measure 4½" x 4½". Make 32 blocks.

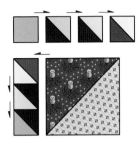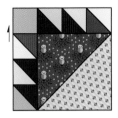

Make 32.

Assembling and Finishing the Quilt

1 Arrange the blocks, side triangles, and corner triangles in diagonal rows. Sew the blocks and side triangles in diagonal rows. Join the rows and add the oversized corner triangles on each corner. Press the seam allowances as indicated. Trim the corner triangles ¼" beyond the corner of the blocks.

Quilt assembly

2 Measure the length of the quilt top, cut two brown 1"-wide strips to this length, and sew them to the sides of the quilt. Press the seam allowances toward the border strips. Measure the width of the quilt top. Cut two brown 1"-wide strips to this length and sew them to the top and bottom of the quilt.

Press the seam allowances toward the border strips. For the pieced border to fit correctly, the quilt top should be 24½" x 30½". Trim the quilt top as needed to get this measurement.

3 Sew the remaining light and dark 1⅞" triangles together. Press the seam allowances toward the dark triangles. Make 108 units. Sew 24 half-square-triangle units together, orienting the dark triangles in the same direction. Make two borders for the top and bottom of the quilt. Sew 30 half-square-triangle units together in the same manner. Sew a brown 1½" square to each end of the 30-unit border. Make two side borders.

Make 2.

Make 2.

4 Sew the top and bottom borders to the quilt top, orienting the dark triangles toward the center of the quilt. Press the seam allowances toward the 1"-wide border. Sew the side borders to the quilt top in the same manner.

Quilt plan

5 Layer the backing, batting, and quilt top. Baste, and then quilt as desired.

6 Attach the brown 2¼"-wide binding strips.

Up North, Down South

This block is sometimes known as Broken Band, but we like to call it Up North, Down South, as it points in all directions. Whether you're from the North or the South, you will enjoy this quilt stitched in a palette of soft reds, navy blues, and creams.

Quilt size: 49½" x 63½"
Finished block: 7" x 7"

Materials

Yardages are based on 42"-wide fabric.

½ yard *each* of 8 light cream and ivory prints for blocks and setting squares

¼ yard *each* of 8 medium blue, pink, red, black, and tan prints for blocks

¼ yard *each* of 8 dark blue, pink, red, black, and tan prints for blocks

½ yard of dark blue print for binding

3¼ yards of fabric for backing (pieced horizontally)

53" x 67" piece of batting

Cutting

Measurements include ¼"-wide seam allowances.

From the light prints, cut:

31 squares, 7½" x 7½"

32 squares, 3" x 3"

32 sets of 8 matching connector squares, 1¾" x 1¾" (256 total)

32 sets of 4 matching squares, 1¾" x 1¾" (128 total)

From the dark prints, cut:

64 squares, 2⅝" x 2⅝"; cut squares in half diagonally to yield 32 sets of 4 matching triangles (128 total)

32 sets of 8 matching rectangles, 1¾" x 3" (256 total)

From the medium prints, cut:

64 squares, 3" x 3"; cut squares into quarters diagonally to yield 32 sets of 8 matching triangles (256 total)

32 sets of 8 matching connector squares, 1¾" x 1¾" (256 total)

From the dark blue print, cut:

6 strips, 2¼" x 42"

Making the Up North, Down South Blocks

Use one light, one medium, and one dark print for each block.

1 Draw a diagonal line on the wrong side of each light 1¾" connector square. Place a marked square on one end of a dark 1¾" x 3" rectangle, right sides together. Sew on the drawn line. Trim the outside corner *of the connector square only,* ¼" from the stitching line. Press the seam allowances toward the corner. Repeat on the other end of the rectangle. Make four light units.

Make 4.

2 Referring to step 1, sew two medium 1¾" connector squares to a dark 1¾" x 3" rectangle. Press the seam allowances toward the corners. Make four medium units.

Make 4.

3 Join the four light units from step 1, the four medium units from step 2, a light 3" square, four light 1¾" squares, eight medium 3" triangles, and four dark 2⅝" triangles. Press the seam allowances as indicated. The block should measure 7½" x 7½". Make 32 blocks.

 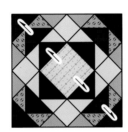

Make 32.

Assembling and Finishing the Quilt

1 Arrange the blocks, alternating pieced blocks and light 7½" squares in nine rows. Sew the blocks in rows. Press the seam allowances toward the light squares. Join the rows. Press the seam allowances in one direction.

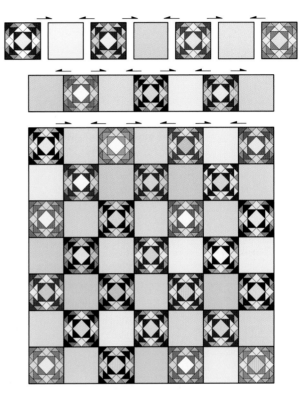

Quilt assembly

2 Layer the backing, batting, and quilt top. Baste, and then quilt as desired.
3 Attach the dark blue 2¼"-wide binding strips.

Battlefield

W hether Union or Confederate, hundreds of thousands of soldiers marched across farm fields and fallow lands in 23 states and several territories, waging war in more than 100 battles during the course of the American Civil War. The crisscrossing pattern of this quilt, made from simple stars and Hourglass blocks, mimics the paths these soldiers took and commemorates the lives lost during this war.

Quilt size: 55½" x 65½"
Finished blocks: Hourglass block: 5" x 5"
Star block: 5" x 5"

Materials

Yardages are based on 42"-wide fabric.
¼ yard *each* of 14 medium and dark prints for Hourglass blocks
⅛ yard *each* of 8 light prints for Star blocks
⅛ yard *each* of 8 dark prints for Star blocks
⅜ yard of medium-light print #1 for spacer blocks
½ yard of medium-light print #2 for spacer blocks
½ yard of dark brown print for binding
3¾ yards of fabric for backing (pieced horizontally)
59" x 69" piece of batting

Cutting

Measurements include ¼"-wide seam allowances.

Cutting for 4 Center Hourglass Blocks
From *1* of the dark prints, cut:
2 squares, 6¼" x 6¼"; cut squares into quarters diagonally to yield 8 triangles

From *1* of the medium prints, cut:
2 squares, 6¼" x 6¼"; cut squares into quarters diagonally to yield 8 triangles

Cutting for Remaining Hourglass Blocks
From the remaining medium and dark prints, cut:
68 squares, 6¼" x 6¼"; cut squares into quarters diagonally to yield 272 triangles

Cutting for Star Blocks
From the dark prints, cut:
31 squares, 2½" x 2½"
31 sets of 8 matching connector squares, 1½" x 1½" (248 total)

From the light prints, cut:
31 sets of 4 matching rectangles, 2" x 2½" (124 total)
31 sets of 4 matching squares, 2" x 2" (124 total)

Cutting for Spacer Blocks
From medium-light print #1, cut:
16 squares, 5½" x 5½"

From medium-light print #2, cut:
24 squares, 5½" x 5½"

Cutting for Binding
From the dark brown print, cut:
6 strips, 2¼" x 42"

Making the Hourglass Blocks

1 Use one medium and one dark print for all four of the center blocks. Join a dark 6¼" triangle and a medium 6¼" triangle along their short edges. Press the seam allowances toward the dark triangle. Make two. Sew the two units together to make an Hourglass block. The block should measure 5½" x 5½". Make four identical blocks; these will be used to form the star in the center of the quilt.

Make 4.

2 For the remaining Hourglass blocks, sew four different 6¼" triangles together, mixing and matching medium and dark prints as desired. Press. Make 68 blocks.

Make 68.

Making the Star Blocks

Use one light and one dark print for each block.

1 Draw a diagonal line on the wrong side of each dark 1½" connector square. Place a marked square on a light 2" x 2½" rectangle, right sides together. Sew on the drawn line. Trim the outside corner *of the connector square only,* ¼" from the stitching line. Press the seam allowances toward the corner. Repeat on the other end of the rectangle. Make four units.

Make 4.

2 Join the four units from step 1, a dark 2½" square, and four light 2" squares. Press the seam allowances as indicated. The block should measure 5½" x 5½". Make 31 blocks.

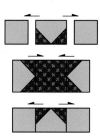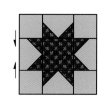

Make 31.

Assembling and Finishing the Quilt

1 Arrange the Star blocks, Hourglass blocks, and spacer blocks in horizontal rows. Note that the two prints for the spacer blocks alternate diagonally around the center set of stars. Sew the blocks together in rows. Press the seam allowances toward the Hourglass blocks. Join the rows. Press the seam allowances in one direction.

Quilt assembly

2 Layer the backing, batting, and quilt top. Baste, and then quilt as desired.
3 Attach the dark brown 2¼"-wide binding strips.

Civil War Log Cabin

No quilt block is more American than the humble Log Cabin. In this version, we arranged the blocks with the strong dark-and-light diagonal shading in a straight furrows set, which seemed appropriate for all the farmers and farmhands who fought side by side on our nation's farmlands.

Quilt size: 50" x 66½"
Finished block: 8¼" x 8¼"

Materials

Yardages are based on 42"-wide fabric.
⅛ yard *each* of 18 light prints for blocks
⅛ yard *each* of 18 medium-light prints for blocks
⅛ yard *each* of 18 medium-dark prints for blocks
⅛ yard *each* of 18 dark prints for blocks
⅛ yard of red fabric for block centers
½ yard of black fabric for binding
3⅓ yards of fabric for backing (pieced horizontally)
54" x 70" piece of batting

Cutting

Measurements include ¼"-wide seam allowances.
Cutting instructions for Log Cabin blocks are
provided at right and on page 21.
From the black fabric, cut:
6 strips, 2¼" x 42"

Making the Log Cabin Blocks

The blocks are made up of rotary-cut pieces, which are indicated by number in the chart at right and on page 21. There are two different blocks: In 24 of the blocks, the last round uses a dark strip and a light strip. In the other 24 blocks, the last round uses a medium-dark strip and a medium-light strip.

We sewed our blocks one at a time, choosing fabric as we went, rather than chain piecing them. Note that in each block there are only four different fabrics plus the red center. Of those four different fabrics, each starts as a strip cut 1¼" x 42". The strips are then cut to make each log. Join each log to the block in the order given, pressing the seam allowances toward the log just added.

Log Cabin Block 1 (Ending with a Dark Log and a Light Log)

Cutting instructions are for 1 block. Make 24.

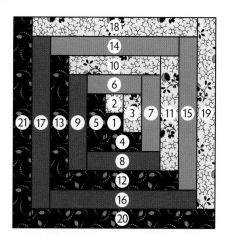

PIECE	FABRIC	CUTTING
1	red	1¼" x 1¼"
2	light	1¼" x 1¼"
3	light	1¼" x 2"
4	dark	1¼" x 2"
5	dark	1¼" x 2¾"
6	medium light	1¼" x 2¾"
7	medium light	1¼" x 3½"
8	medium dark	1¼" x 3½"
9	medium dark	1¼" x 4¼"
10	light	1¼" x 4¼"
11	light	1¼" x 5"
12	dark	1¼" x 5"
13	dark	1¼" x 5¾"
14	medium light	1¼" x 5¾"
15	medium light	1¼" x 6½"
16	medium dark	1¼" x 6½"
17	medium dark	1¼" x 7¼"
18	light	1¼" x 7¼"
19	light	1¼" x 8"
20	dark	1¼" x 8"
21	dark	1¼" x 8¾"

Log Cabin Block 2 (Ending with a Medium-Dark Log and a Medium-Light Log)

Cutting instructions are for 1 block. Make 24.

PIECE	FABRIC	CUTTING
1	red	1¼" x 1¼"
2	medium light	1¼" x 1¼"
3	medium light	1¼" x 2"
4	medium dark	1¼" x 2"
5	medium dark	1¼" x 2¾"
6	light	1¼" x 2¾"
7	light	1¼" x 3½"
8	dark	1¼" x 3½"
9	dark	1¼" x 4¼"
10	medium light	1¼" x 4¼"
11	medium light	1¼" x 5"
12	medium dark	1¼" x 5"
13	medium dark	1¼" x 5¾"
14	light	1¼" x 5¾"
15	light	1¼" x 6½"
16	dark	1¼" x 6½"
17	dark	1¼" x 7¼"
18	medium light	1¼" x 7¼"
19	medium light	1¼" x 8"
20	medium dark	1¼" x 8"
21	medium dark	1¼" x 8¾"

Assembling and Finishing the Quilt

1 Arrange the blocks in eight rows of six blocks each, alternating blocks 1 and 2, and rotating the blocks to form the diagonal pattern of lights and darks.

2 Sew the blocks together in rows, pressing the seam allowances in opposite directions from row to row. Join the rows. Press the seam allowances in one direction.

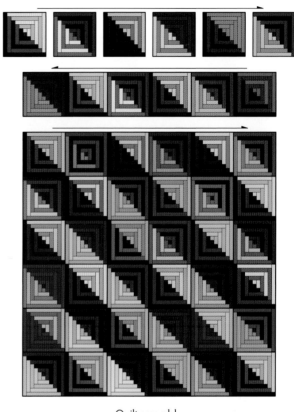

Quilt assembly

3 Layer the backing, batting, and quilt top. Baste, and then quilt as desired.

4 Attach the black 2¼"-wide binding strips.

Ohio Star Crossing

Ohio was a state divided during the Civil War. The northern portion of the state supplied much-needed troops and cash to the Union army, while southern Ohio's alliances leaned more toward the Confederacy. Two minor battles took place in Ohio, and a camp near Sandusky by Lake Erie housed Confederate prisoners of war.

Quilt size: 42½" x 54½"
Finished blocks: Ohio Star block: 6" x 6"
Checkerboard block: 6" x 6"

Materials

Yardages are based on 42"-wide fabric.
¼ yard *each* of 6 assorted light prints for spacer blocks
1 yard *total* of assorted scraps in dark blue, red, brown, and black prints for Ohio Star and Checkerboard blocks
½ yard *total* of assorted scraps in cream and ivory prints for Ohio Star blocks
½ yard *total* of assorted scraps in medium gray, tan, brown, and blue prints for Ohio Star blocks
½ yard *total* of assorted scraps in light cream, red, tan, and taupe prints for Checkerboard blocks
½ yard of dark print for bias binding
2¾ yards of fabric for backing (pieced horizontally)
46" x 58" piece of batting

Cutting

Measurements include ¼"-wide seam allowances.
From the assorted scraps of dark blue, red, brown, and black prints, cut:
18 sets of 2 matching squares, 3¼" x 3¼" (36 total); cut squares into quarters diagonally to yield 18 sets of 8 matching triangles (144 total)
18 squares, 2½" x 2½"
252 squares, 1½" x 1½"

From the assorted scraps of cream and ivory prints, cut:
18 sets of 2 matching squares, 3¼" x 3¼" (36 total); cut squares into quarters diagonally to yield 18 sets of 8 matching triangles (144 total)

From the assorted scraps of medium gray, brown, and blue prints, cut:
18 sets of 4 matching squares, 2½" x 2½" (72 total)

From the assorted scraps of light cream, red, tan, and taupe prints, cut:
252 squares, 1½" x 1½"

From the 6 assorted ¼-yard light prints, cut:
31 squares, 6½" x 6½"

From the dark print, cut:
2¼"-wide bias strips, enough to yield 200" of binding

Making the Ohio Star Blocks

You can use one light, one medium, and one dark print for each block, or mix some of them up as we did.

1 Join two cream or ivory 3¼" triangles and two dark 3¼" triangles. Press the seam allowances as indicated. Make four units.

Make 4.

2 Join the four units from step 1, four medium 2½" squares, and one dark 2½" square. Press the seam allowances as indicated. The block should measure 6½" x 6½". Make 18 blocks.

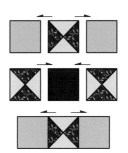 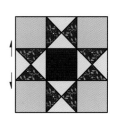

Make 18.

Making the Checkerboard Blocks

1 Arrange 18 light 1½" squares and 18 dark 1½" squares into six rows of six squares each, alternating light and dark squares from row to row, and using the same print in each diagonal row.

2 Sew the squares together. Press the seam allowances toward the dark squares. Join the rows. Press the seam allowances in one direction. The block should measure 6½" x 6½". Make 14 blocks.

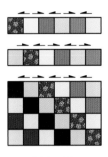

Make 14.

Assembling and Finishing the Quilt

1 Arrange the Ohio Star blocks, Checkerboard blocks, and spacer blocks into nine rows, placing the Ohio Star blocks in the center and the Checkerboard blocks around the outside. Sew the blocks in rows. Press the seam allowances toward the spacer blocks. Join the rows. Press the seam allowances in one direction.

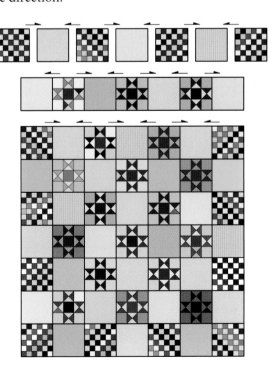

Quilt assembly

2 You can leave the quilt top square, or round the corners as we did. Place a 5"-diameter plate or cardboard circle on the corner block and trace the curve. Trim the corner on the drawn line.

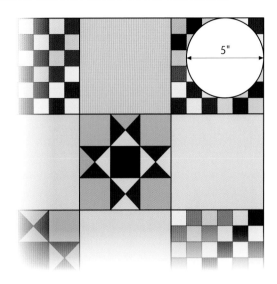

3 Layer the backing, batting, and quilt top. Baste, and then quilt as desired.

4 Attach the dark 2¼"-wide bias-binding strips.

Broken Dishes

Quilt blocks were often named after common household items and everyday things. During the course of the Civil War, much more than dishes were broken when sons, brothers, fathers, and uncles marched off to battle.

Quilt size: 36½" x 36½"
Finished block: 6" x 6"

Materials
Yardages are based on 42"-wide fabric.
1½ yards *total* of assorted light prints for blocks and sashing pieces
1½ yards *total* of assorted medium and dark prints for blocks
⅓ yard of red print for binding
1¼ yards of fabric for backing
40" x 40" piece of batting

Cutting
Measurements include ¼"-wide seam allowances.

Cutting for 1 Broken Dishes Block
From *1* of the assorted light prints, cut:
1 square, 3¼" x 3¼"; cut square into quarters diagonally to yield 4 triangles
6 squares, 1⅞" x 1⅞"; cut squares in half diagonally to yield 12 triangles
4 rectangles, 1½" x 2½"

From *1* of the assorted medium or dark prints, cut:
2 squares, 2⅞" x 2⅞"; cut squares in half diagonally to yield 4 triangles
1 square, 2½" x 2½"
6 squares, 1⅞" x 1⅞"; cut squares in half diagonally to yield 12 triangles

Cutting for Sashing and Stars
From the assorted light prints, cut:
40 rectangles, 2" x 6½"

From the assorted medium and dark prints, cut:
16 squares, 2" x 2"
8 matching connector squares, 1¼" x 1¼", to match each 2" square (128 total)

Cutting for Binding
From the red print, cut:
4 strips, 2¼" x 42"

Making the Broken Dishes Blocks
Use one light and one dark (or medium) print for each block.

1 Sew four light 3¼" triangles to the sides of a dark 2½" square. Press the seam allowances toward the dark square.

2 Sew four dark 2⅞" triangles to the sides of the unit from step 1. Press the seam allowances toward the dark triangles.

3 Sew a light 1⅞" triangle to a dark 1⅞" triangle to make a half-square-triangle unit. Make 12 units.

Make 12.

4 Join four light 1½" x 2½" rectangles, the unit from step 2, and the 12 units from step 3. Press the seam allowances as indicated. The block should measure 6½" x 6½". Make 25 blocks.

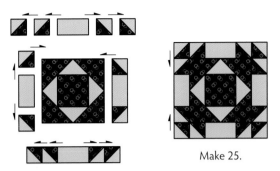

Make 25.

Assembling and Finishing the Quilt

1 Draw a diagonal line on the wrong side of each dark 1¼" connector square.

2 Arrange five Broken Dishes blocks and four light 2" x 6½" sashing rectangles in each of five rows. Arrange five light 2" x 6½" sashing rectangles and four dark 2" squares in alternating rows. When you have a pleasing arrangement, pin a marked connector square to each corner of the 24 sashing rectangles in the quilt center, right sides together, making sure the connector squares match the adjacent 2" dark squares. Pin two connector squares to each of the 16 sashing rectangles around the perimeter of the quilt. Again, the pieces in each star should be the same fabric.

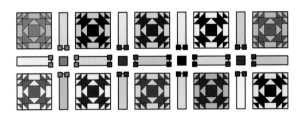

3 Sew on the drawn line of one of the connector squares. Trim the outside corner *of the connector square only*, ¼" from the stitching line. Press the seam allowances toward the corner. Repeat with remaining squares pinned on all rectangles.

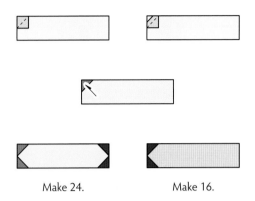

Make 24.   Make 16.

4 Sew the blocks and sashing units together in rows. Press the seam allowances toward the sashing units. Sew the sashing units and 2" dark squares together in rows. Press the seam allowances toward the sashing units. Join the rows. Press the seam allowances toward the sashing rows.

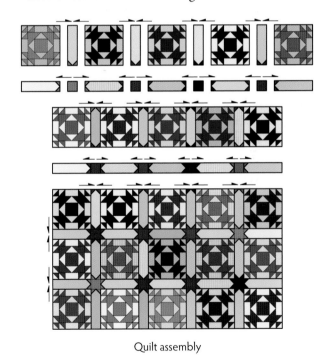

Quilt assembly

5 Layer the backing, batting, and quilt top. Baste, and then quilt as desired.

6 Attach the red 2¼"-wide binding strips.

Blue stars, both dark and light, sparkle across the surface of this patriotic small quilt, which can do double duty as a table runner.

Quilt size: 20½" x 36½"
Finished blocks: Four-patch unit: 2" x 2"
Star and Hourglass blocks: 4" x 4"

Materials

Yardages are based on 42"-wide fabric.

1 yard *total* of assorted light prints for Star blocks, Hourglass blocks, and four-patch units

1 yard *total* of assorted medium and dark blue prints for Star blocks, Hourglass blocks, and four-patch units

2 squares, 6" x 6", of medium and dark brown prints for Hourglass blocks

¼ yard *each* of 2 dark red prints for Star block, Hourglass blocks, four-patch units, and border corner squares

¼ yard of dark blue print for border

¼ yard of red print for binding

1⅛ yards of fabric for backing

24" x 40" piece of batting

Cutting

Measurements include ¼"-wide seam allowances.

Cutting for 16 Dark Star Blocks
From the assorted medium and dark blue prints, cut:
16 squares, 2½" x 2½"
16 sets of 8 matching connector squares, 1½" x 1½", to match each 2½" square (128 total)

From the assorted light prints, cut:
16 sets of 4 matching rectangles, 1½" x 2½" (68 total)
16 sets of 4 matching squares, 1½" x 1½" (68 total)

Cutting for 1 Light Star Block
From *1* of the light prints, cut:
1 square, 2½" x 2½"
8 connector squares, 1½" x 1½"

From *1* of the dark red prints, cut:
4 rectangles, 1½" x 2½"
4 squares, 1½" x 1½"

Cutting for Hourglass Blocks
From the assorted light prints, cut:
6 squares, 5¼" x 5¼"; cut squares into quarters diagonally to yield 24 triangles

From the assorted medium and dark blue prints, cut:
2 squares, 5¼" x 5¼"; cut squares into quarters diagonally to yield 8 triangles

From *each* of the brown prints, cut:
1 square, 5¼" x 5¼"; cut squares into quarters diagonally to yield 4 triangles (8 total)

From *each* of the dark red prints, cut:
1 square, 5¼" x 5¼"; cut square into quarters diagonally to yield 4 triangles (8 total)

Cutting for Four-Patch Units
From the assorted light prints, cut:
32 squares, 1½" x 1½"

From the assorted medium and dark blue prints, cut:
24 squares, 1½" x 1½"

From *1* of the dark red prints, cut:
8 squares, 1½" x 1½"

Cutting for Borders
From the dark blue print, cut:
4 rectangles, 2½" x 15½"
4 rectangles, 2½" x 7½"

From *1* of the dark red prints, cut:
4 squares, 2½" x 2½"

Cutting for Binding
From the red print, cut:
3 strips, 2¼" x 42"

Making the Star Blocks

Use one light and one dark (or medium) print for each block.

1 Draw a diagonal line on the wrong side of each dark blue 1½" connector square. Place a marked square on a light 1½" x 2½" rectangle, right sides together. Sew on the drawn line. Trim the outside corner *of the connector square only,* ¼" from the stitching line. Press the seam allowances toward the corner. Repeat on the other end of the rectangle. Make four units.

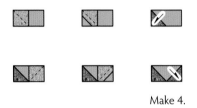

Make 4.

2 Join the four units from step 1, four light 1½" squares, and one dark blue 2½" square. Press the seam allowances as indicated. The block should measure 4½" x 4½". Make 16 blocks.

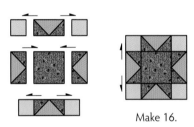

Make 16.

3 Referring to steps 1 and 2, make the center Star block using one light print and one dark red print. Reverse the position of the light and dark prints when making the block.

Make 1.

Making the Hourglass Blocks

Use one light and one dark (or medium) print for each block.

Join two light 5¼" triangles and two dark 5¼" triangles to make an Hourglass block. Press the seam allowances as indicated. The block should measure 4½" x 4½". Make four blue, four brown, and four red blocks.

Make 4 blue, 4 brown, and 4 red blocks.

Making the Four-Patch Units

1 Join two light 1½" squares and two medium or dark blue 1½" squares. Make 12 units.

2 Join two light 1½" squares and two dark red 1½" squares. Make four units.

Make 12.   Make 4.

Assembling and Finishing the Quilt

1 Join the center Star block and the 12 blue four-patch units. Press the seam allowances as indicated.

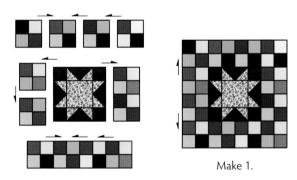

Make 1.

2 Arrange the center unit from step 1, the remaining Star blocks, and the Hourglass blocks, alternating the light and dark triangles in the Hourglass blocks. Sew the blocks in rows. Press the seam allowances as indicated. Join the rows. Press the seam allowances in one direction.

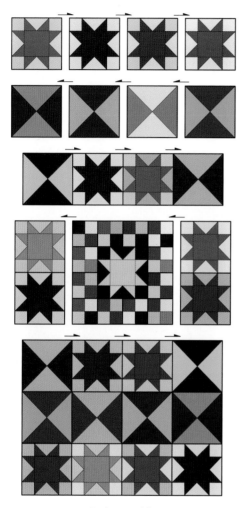

Quilt assembly

3 Sew one red four-patch unit between two dark blue 2½" x 7½" rectangles. Press the seam allowances toward the rectangles. Make two borders for the top and bottom of the quilt. Sew one red four-patch unit between two dark blue 2½" x 15½" rectangles. Sew a red 2½" square to each end. Press

the seam allowances toward the rectangles. Make two side borders.

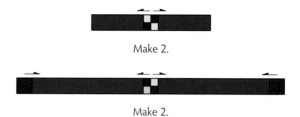

Make 2.

Make 2.

4 Sew the top and bottom borders to the quilt top. Press the seam allowances toward the borders. Sew the side borders to the quilt top. Press the seam allowances toward the borders.

Quilt plan

5 Layer the backing, batting, and quilt top. Baste, and then quilt as desired.

6 Attach the red 2¼"-wide binding strips.

Gettysburg

We named this charming little basket quilt after a town in southern Pennsylvania. Gettysburg was the site of both the Civil War's deadliest battle and President Lincoln's famed address to the nation. Pieced in our version of butternut and blue, we pay homage to the soldiers who died at this important battle site.

Quilt size: 28½" x 36½"
Finished block: 5" x 5"

Materials

Yardages are based on 42"-wide fabric.

1⅞ yards of navy fabric for blocks, setting triangles, borders, and bias binding

¼ yard *each* of 4 gold prints for blocks and inner border

⅛ yard *each* of 6 light and medium blue prints for blocks

⅛ yard *each* of 2 purple prints for blocks

1 yard of fabric for backing

32" x 40" piece of batting

Cutting

Measurements include ¼"-wide seam allowances.

Cutting for 1 Basket Block

From *1* of the gold prints, cut:

1 square, 3⅞" x 3⅞"; cut square in half diagonally to yield 2 triangles. You will use only 1 per block. Use the other triangle for another block.

5 squares, 1⅞" x 1⅞"; cut squares in half diagonally to yield 10 triangles. You will have 1 left over.

From the navy fabric, cut:

1 square, 2⅞" x 2⅞"; cut square in half diagonally to yield 2 triangles. You will use only 1 per block. Use the other triangle for another block.

2 rectangles, 1½" x 3½"

4 squares, 1⅞" x 1⅞"; cut squares in half diagonally to yield 8 triangles. You will have 1 left over.

From *1* of the medium blue prints, cut:

3 squares, 1⅞" x 1⅞"; cut squares in half diagonally to yield 6 triangles

From *1* of the purple or light blue prints, cut:

2 squares, 1⅞" x 1⅞"; cut squares in half diagonally to yield 4 triangles. You will have 1 left over.

Cutting for Setting Pieces, Borders, and Binding

From the remaining navy fabric, cut:

3 squares, 9" x 9"; cut squares into quarters diagonally to yield 12 side triangles.* You will have 2 left over.

2 squares, 6½" x 6½"; cut squares in half diagonally to yield 4 corner triangles*

6 squares, 5½" x 5½"

3 strips, 1⅞" x 42"; cut into 52 squares, 1⅞" x 1⅞". Cut squares in half diagonally to yield 104 triangles.

2 strips, 3" x 23½"

2 strips, 3" x 36½"

2¼"-wide bias strips, enough to yield 150" of binding

**The side and corner triangles are slightly oversized and will be trimmed later.*

From the gold prints, cut:

52 squares, 1⅞" x 1⅞"; cut squares in half diagonally to yield 104 triangles

Making the Basket Blocks

Use one gold print, one light blue (or purple) print, one medium blue print, and navy fabric for each block.

1 Sew a gold 1⅞" triangle to a navy 1⅞" triangle. Press the seam allowances toward the navy triangle. Make seven.

Make 7.

2 Sew a medium blue 1⅞" triangle to a light blue or purple 1⅞" triangle. Press the seam allowances toward the medium blue triangle. Make three.

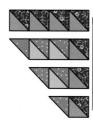

Make 3.

3 Join the seven units from step 1, the three units from step 2, and three medium blue 1⅞" triangles. Press the seam allowances as indicated.

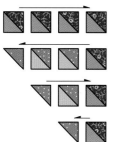

4 Sew a gold 3⅞" triangle to the unit from step 3. Press the seam allowances toward the gold triangle.

5 Sew a gold 1⅞" triangle to the short end of a navy 1½" x 3½" rectangle. Press the seam allowances toward the rectangle. Make two, orienting each triangle as shown.

6 Sew the units from step 5 to adjacent sides of the unit from step 4. Press the seam allowances toward the rectangles. Sew a navy 2⅞" triangle to the remaining corner of the unit. Press the seam allowances toward the center of the block. The block should measure 5½" x 5½". Make 12 blocks.

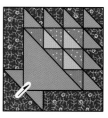
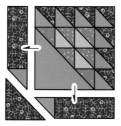

Make 12.

Assembling and Finishing the Quilt

1 Arrange the blocks, navy 5½" squares, side triangles, and corner triangles in diagonal rows. Sew the blocks, squares, and side triangles in rows. Join the rows and add the corner triangles last. Press the seam allowances as indicated. Trim the oversized triangles all around, leaving an equal amount from the block corners so the quilt top measures 21½" x 29½". You'll need this size for the pieced triangle border to fit properly.

Quilt assembly

2 Join the navy 1⅞" triangles and gold 1⅞" triangles. Press the seam allowances toward the navy triangles. Make 104 units. Sew 21 half-square-triangle units together, orienting the navy triangles in the same direction. Make two borders for the top and bottom of the quilt. Sew 31 half-square-triangle units together, orienting the navy triangles in the same direction, except for the last unit, which is turned 90° clockwise. Make two side borders.

Make 2.

Make 2.

3 Sew the top and bottom borders to the quilt top, orienting the light triangles toward the center of the quilt. Press the seam allowances toward the center of the quilt. Sew the side borders to the quilt top in the same manner. The quilt should measure 23½" x 31½".

4 Sew the navy 3" x 23½" border strips to the top and bottom of the quilt. Press the seam allowances toward the border strips. Sew the navy 3" x 36½" border strips to the sides of the quilt. Press the seam allowances toward the border strips.

5 You can leave the quilt top square, or round the corners as we did. Place a 5"-diameter plate or cardboard circle on the corner and trace the curve. Trim the corner on the drawn line.

6 Layer the backing, batting, and quilt top. Baste, and then quilt as desired.

7 Attach the navy 2¼"-wide bias-binding strips.

Quilt plan

Churn Dash Weave

H ere's another old-time block named for a common household item—a butter churn. But what's a churn dash? Well, apparently *dash* signifies the sound of plunking or, in this case, the sound of the slurping that the plunger made when pounded into and pulled out of the butter churn. Here, the unifying light fabric weaves all the blocks together, much like a mended nation.

Quilt size: 35½" x 45½"
Finished block: 5" x 5"

Materials
Yardages are based on 42"-wide fabric.
1¾ yards *total* assorted scraps of dark prints for blocks
1 yard *total* assorted scraps of medium prints for blocks
¾ yard *total* assorted scraps of light prints for blocks
⅓ yard of navy solid for binding*
1½ yards of fabric for backing
39" x 49" piece of batting
We used blue velveteen for binding.

Cutting
Measurements include ¼"-wide seam allowances.

Cutting for 1 Churn Dash Block
From *1* of the dark prints, cut:
2 squares, 2⅞" x 2⅞"; cut squares in half diagonally to yield 4 triangles
4 squares, 1½" x 1½"

From *1* of the medium prints, cut:
2 squares, 2⅞" x 2⅞"; cut squares in half diagonally to yield 4 triangles

From *1* of the light prints, cut:
5 squares, 1½" x 1½"

Cutting for Binding
From the navy solid, cut:
5 strips, 2¼" x 42"

Making the Churn Dash Blocks
Use one light, one medium, and one dark print for each block.

1 Sew a medium 2⅞" triangle to a dark 2⅞" triangle. Press the seam allowances toward the dark triangle. Make four units.

Make 4.

2 Sew a light 1½" square to a dark 1½" square. Press the seam allowances toward the dark square. Make two units. Sew three light 1½" squares and two dark 1½" squares into a row. Press the seam allowances toward the dark squares.

Make 2.   Make 1.

3 Sew the units from steps 1 and 2 together. Press the seam allowances as indicated. The block should measure 5½" x 5½". Make 63 blocks.

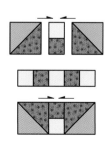 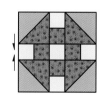

Make 63.

Assembling and Finishing the Quilt

1 Arrange the blocks in nine rows of seven blocks each. Sew the blocks together in rows, pressing the seam allowances in opposite directions from row to row. Join the rows. Press the seam allowances in one direction.

2 Layer the backing, batting, and quilt top. Baste, and then quilt as desired.

3 Attach the navy 2¼"-wide binding strips.

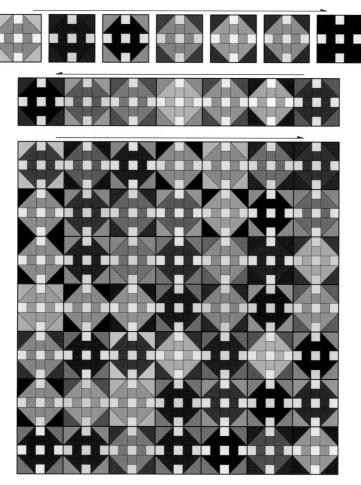

Quilt assembly

So many letters between soldiers and their families were written during the Civil War. It's hard to imagine how they were ever delivered! Diaries and journals were also kept, perhaps to help pass the time until news of a loved one arrived. These Journal blocks commemorate that discipline of keeping track. While these blocks look complex, each of the 16 pieces in the block is cut exactly the same, making quick work of that task.

Quilt size: 36½" x 36½"
Finished block: Journal block: 6" x 6"
Hourglass block: 3" x 3"

Materials

Yardages are based on 42"-wide fabric.
2 yards *total* assorted scraps of ivory, cream, gold, gray, black, navy, red, and pink prints for blocks
⅓ yard of gray print for binding
1¼ yards of fabric for backing
40" x 40" piece of batting

Cutting

Measurements include ¼"-wide seam allowances.
From the assorted prints, cut:
144 squares, 4¼" x 4¼"; cut squares into quarters diagonally to yield 576 triangles
Note: You can use the same prints in a block, or mix some of them up as we did. For matched pieces, you will need two triangles for piece #1, two triangles for piece #2, six triangles for piece #3, and six triangles for piece #4 (16 total for each block).

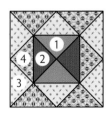

From the gray print, cut:
4 strips, 2¼" x 42"

Making the Journal Blocks

Arrange and sew 16 triangles into quarter sections. Sew two quarters together to make a half section, and then sew two halves together. The block should measure 6½" x 6½". Make 25 blocks.

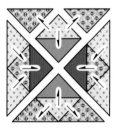
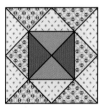

Make 25.

Making the Hourglass Blocks

Use one light and one contrasting print for each block. Join two light triangles and two dark triangles to make an Hourglass block. Press the seam allowances as indicated. The block should measure 3½" x 3½". Make 44 blocks.

Make 44.

Assembling and Finishing the Quilt

1 Arrange the Journal blocks in five rows of five blocks each, rotating the blocks so the light and medium triangles alternate positions from block to block. Sew the blocks together in rows, pressing the seam allowances in opposite directions from row to row. Join the rows. Press the seam allowances in one direction.

Quilt assembly

2 Arrange and join 10 Hourglass blocks, rotating the blocks so the light and dark triangles alternate positions from block to block. Press the seam allowances toward the darker triangles. Make two borders for the top and bottom of the quilt. Sew 12 border blocks together in the same manner to make two side borders.

Make 2.

Make 2.

3 Sew the top and bottom borders to the quilt top. Press the seam allowances toward the borders. Sew the side borders to the quilt top. Press the seam allowances toward the borders.

Quilt plan

4 Layer the backing, batting, and quilt top. Baste, and then quilt as desired.

5 Attach the gray 2¼"-wide binding strips.

A lbum blocks were quite popular in the 1800s. The light centers of the blocks were a place to gather signatures. In this scrappy version, the blocks interlock with splashes of red that form pinwheels.

Quilt size: 37½" x 47½"
Finished blocks: Album block: 7" x 7"
Pinwheel block: 3" x 3"

Materials

Yardages are based on 42"-wide fabric.
1⅓ yards of muslin for blocks
1⅛ yards *total* assorted scraps of dark prints for blocks
⅝ yard *total* assorted scraps of light prints for blocks
½ yard *total* assorted scraps of red prints for
    Pinwheel blocks
⅜ yard of dark blue print for binding
1⅝ yards of fabric for backing
41" x 51" piece of batting

Cutting

Measurements include ¼"-wide seam allowances.

Cutting for 1 Album Block
From *1* of the dark prints, cut:
4 rectangles, 1½" x 3½"
8 squares, 1½" x 1½"

From the muslin, cut:
4 squares, 2½" x 2½"
8 squares, 1½" x 1½"

From *1* of the light prints, cut:
1 rectangle, 1½" x 3½"
2 squares, 1½" x 1½"

Cutting for 1 Segmented Album Block
From *1* of the dark prints, cut:
4 rectangles, 1½" x 3½"
8 squares, 1½" x 1½"

From *1* of the light prints, cut:
1 rectangle, 1½" x 3½"
2 squares, 1½" x 1½"

From the muslin, cut:
8 squares, 1½" x 1½"

Cutting for 1 Pinwheel Block
From *1* of the red prints, cut:
2 squares, 2⅜" x 2⅜"; cut squares in half diagonally
    to yield 4 triangles
From the muslin, cut:
2 squares, 2⅜" x 2⅜"; cut squares in half diagonally
    to yield 4 triangles

Cutting for Background Rectangles
From the muslin, cut:
14 rectangles, 2½" x 3½"

Cutting for Binding
From the dark blue print, cut:
5 strips, 2¼" x 42"

Making the Album Blocks

Use one light print, one dark print, and muslin for each block.

1 Sew a dark 1½" square between two muslin 1½" squares. Press the seam allowances toward the dark square. Then sew a dark 1½" x 3½" rectangle to the unit. Press the seam allowances toward the rectangle. Make four side units.

Make 4.

2 Sew a light 1½" square between two dark 1½" squares. Press the seam allowances toward the dark squares. Make two units. Sew a light 1½" x 3½" rectangle between the two units just made. Press the seam allowances toward the pieced units. Make one center unit.

Make 1.

3 Join the four side units from step 1, the center unit from step 2, and four muslin 2½" squares. Press the seam allowances as indicated. The block should measure 7½" x 7½". Make 20 blocks.

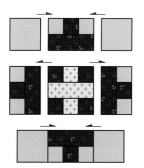
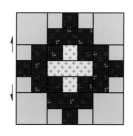

Make 20.

Making the Segmented Album Blocks

1 Repeat steps 1 and 2 for the Album blocks; do not join the units yet.

Side units.
Make 4.

Center unit.
Make 1.

2 Join two side units and one center unit. Press the seam allowances toward the side units. The remaining two side units will be used when arranging the rows. Make 12 blocks.

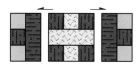

Make 12.

Making the Pinwheel Blocks

1 Join one red 2⅜" triangle and one muslin 2⅜" triangle. Press the seam allowances toward the red triangle. Make four units.

Make 4.

2 Join the four units from step 1. Press the seam allowances as indicated. The block should measure 3½" x 3½". Make 31 blocks.

Make 31.

Assembling and Finishing the Quilt

1 Arrange the Album blocks, Pinwheel blocks, segmented Album blocks, and muslin 2½" x 3½" rectangles in rows. Make sure to place matching segmented Album blocks together. Sew the units between the Album blocks together *before* joining the row. Sew the blocks and units together in rows. Press the seam allowances as indicated. Join the rows. Press the seam allowances in one direction.

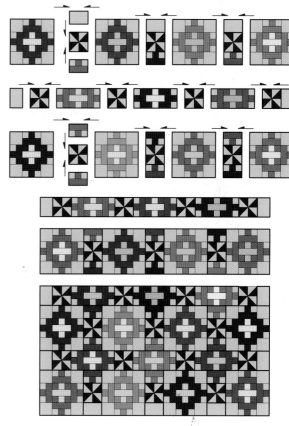

Quilt assembly

2 Layer the backing, batting, and quilt top. Baste, and then quilt as desired.

3 Attach the dark blue 2¼"-wide binding strips.

Blue and Gray

The humble Nine Patch block has been a perennial favorite among quilters for well over a century. While it was first published as a pattern in the late 1800s, it was certainly used well before then, and its simplicity made it perfect for utilitarian quilts that used up scraps. While this version is small, you can see how it could easily be made bed-sized by making larger blocks. More likely, this type of quilt would have been made long and narrow for a "hired man's" cot.

Quilt size: 40¼" x 47¾"
Finished blocks: Red Cross block: 2¾" x 2¾"
Nine Patch block: 5¼" x 5¼"

Materials
Yardages are based on 42"-wide fabric.
⅛ yard *each* of 15 assorted light prints for Nine Patch and Red Cross blocks
⅛ yard *each* of 15 assorted dark blue prints for Nine Patch blocks
⅞ yard of dark blue print for sashing, cornerstones, and bias binding
¼ yard *each* of 5 assorted medium blue and gray prints for sashing
⅛ yard *each* of 5 assorted red prints for Red Cross blocks
2½ yards of fabric for backing (pieced horizontally)
44" x 52" piece of batting

Cutting
Measurements include ¼"-wide seam allowances.
From the assorted light prints, cut:
120 squares, 2¼" x 2¼", for Nine Patch blocks
152 squares, 1¼" x 1¼", for Red Cross blocks

From the assorted dark blue prints, cut:
150 squares, 2¼" x 2¼"

From the assorted red prints, cut:
76 squares, 1¼" x 1¼"
38 rectangles, 1¼" x 2¾"

From the assorted medium blue and gray prints, cut:
49 rectangles, 2¾" x 5¾"

From the dark blue print, cut:
4 strips, 2¾" x 42"; crosscut into:
22 rectangles, 2¾" x 5¾"
4 squares, 2¾" x 2¾"
2¼"-wide bias strips, enough to yield 186" of binding

Making the Nine Patch Blocks
Use four matching light 2¼" squares and five matching dark 2¼" squares for each block.

1 Sew two rows using dark squares on opposite sides of a light square. Make one row with light squares on opposite sides of a dark square.

Make 2.   Make 1.

2 Sew the rows together with the dark/light/dark rows on the top and bottom to complete a Nine Patch block. Press the seam allowances in one direction. The block should measure 5¾" x 5¾". Make 30 blocks.

Nine Patch block.
Make 30.

Making the Red Cross Blocks

Use four matching light 1¼" squares and a matching set of two 1¼" red squares and one red 1¼" x 2¾" rectangle for each block.

1 Sew light squares to opposite sides of a red square. Make two.

Make 2.

2 Sew the matching rows from step 1 to each long side of the red rectangle. Press the seam allowances toward the rectangle. The block should measure 2¼" x 2¼". Make 38 blocks.

Red Cross block.
Make 38.

Assembling and Finishing the Quilt

1 Arrange the Nine Patch blocks in six rows of five blocks each. Place a medium blue or gray rectangle between each block in the rows. Place dark blue rectangles on the outer edges of each row. Sew the blocks and sashing rectangles together to make six block rows. Press the seam allowances toward the rectangles.

Make 6 rows.

2 For the sashing rows between the block rows, place five medium blue or gray rectangles horizontally in a row, separated by Red Cross blocks. Place a Red Cross block on each end of the sashing rows too. Sew the pieces together, and repeat to make five sashing rows. Press the seam allowances toward the rectangles.

Make 5 rows.

3 Make the top and bottom border rows using five dark blue rectangles separated by four Red Cross blocks. Add dark blue squares to the ends of each row. Press the seam allowances toward the dark blue rectangles.

Make 2 borders.

4 Join all rows, starting with a dark blue border row, then alternating the Nine Patch block and sashing rows, and ending with the remaining dark blue border row. Press.

Quilt plan

5 You can leave the quilt top square, or round the corners as we did. Place a 5"-diameter plate or cardboard circle on the corner block and trace the curve as shown on page 25. Trim the corner on the drawn line.

6 Layer the backing, batting, and quilt top. Baste, and then quilt as desired.

7 Attach the dark blue 2¼"-wide bias-binding strips.

While the Pinwheels in this quilt speak to a playful nature and happier times, this scrappy project made of Civil War–era prints also reminds us of a time of making do. Showcase your favorite vintage-inspired prints—the more the merrier—in this anything-goes scrap quilt.

Quilt size: 31½" x 39½"
Finished blocks: Pinwheel block: 4" x 4"
Checkerboard block: 4" x 4"

Materials

Yardage is based on 42"-wide fabric.
¼ yard *each* of 20 assorted dark prints (5 browns, 4 reds, 4 blacks, 4 golds, 1 rose, 1 olive, and 1 teal) for blocks and pieced border
¼ yard *each* of 20 assorted light prints for blocks and pieced border
¼ yard of brown print for inner border
⅜ yard of dark brown print for binding
1¼ yards of fabric for backing
35" x 43" piece of batting

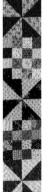

Choosing Fabrics
This project is enhanced by the use of many different fabrics. Twenty assorted fat quarters will get you off to a good start, but feel free to add in others from your stash or scrap basket to create an even scrappier look.

For the light prints, look for small prints that include color or different shades of ivory to tan. Choose shirtings, checks, stripes, and small geometrical designs to give your quilt lots of interest.

Cutting

Measurements include ¼"-wide seam allowances.
From the assorted light prints, cut:
64 squares, 2⅞" x 2⅞"; cut squares in half diagonally to yield 128 triangles
248 squares, 1½" x 1½"
68 squares, 1⅞" x 1⅞"; cut squares in half diagonally to yield 136 triangles

From the assorted dark prints, cut:
64 squares, 2⅞" x 2⅞"; cut squares in half diagonally to yield 128 triangles
248 squares, 1½" x 1½"
68 squares, 1⅞" x 1⅞"; cut squares in half diagonally to yield 136 triangles

From the brown print, cut:
2 strips, 1" x 28½"
2 strips, 1" x 37½"

From the dark brown print, cut:
4 strips, 2¼" x 42"

Making the Pinwheel Blocks

Use four matching light 2⅞" triangles and four matching dark 2⅞" triangles for each block.

1 Join one light and one dark triangle. Press the seam allowances toward the dark triangle. Make four half-square-triangle units.

Make 4 matching.

2 Sew the four triangle units together as shown to make a Pinwheel block. Press the seam allowances as indicated. The block should measure 4½" x 4½". Make 32 blocks.

Make 32.

Making the Checkerboard Blocks

1 Randomly select two light and two dark 1½" squares. Sew them together to make a four-patch unit. Make 124 units.

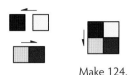

Make 124.

2 Sew four of the assorted four-patch units from step 1 together to make a 16-patch Checkerboard block. Press. The block should measure 4½" x 4½". Make 31 blocks.

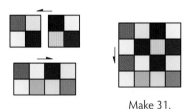

Make 31.

Assembling and Finishing the Quilt

1 Sew a pair of light and dark 1⅞" triangles together. Press the seam allowances toward the dark triangle. Make 136 units.

2 Sew 29 half-square-triangle units together, orienting the dark triangles in the same direction. Make two borders for the top and bottom of the quilt. Sew 39 half-square-triangle units together in the same manner. Make two side borders. Press all seam allowances in the same direction.

Make 2.

Make 2.

3 Alternating Pinwheel and Checkerboard blocks, arrange the blocks in nine rows of seven blocks each. Rearrange until you are pleased with the color placement. Sew the blocks together in rows, pressing the seams allowances in opposite directions from row to row. Join the rows and press the seam allowances in one direction.

4 Sew the 1" x 28½" inner-border strips to the top and bottom of the quilt top. Press the seam allowances toward the border strips. Sew the 1" x 37½" strips to the quilt sides in the same manner.

5 Sew the 29-unit border strips to the top and bottom of the quilt top with the light edge of the strips toward the inner border. Press the seam allowances toward the inner border. Sew the 39-unit strips to the sides of the quilt in the same manner.

Quilt plan

6 Layer the backing, batting, and quilt top. Baste, and then quilt as desired.

7 Attach the dark brown 2¼"-wide binding strips.

Civil Unrest

These days, unfortunately, our country is no stranger to bouts of civil unrest, from peaceful demonstrations to escalated bursts of rioting. However, it's hard to imagine the degree of unrest that occurred when Lincoln was elected president and denounced the right to own slaves, ultimately culminating in the Civil War. This quilt is much more peaceful, don't you think? It's busy, yet orderly!

Quilt size: 35½" x 35½"

Finished blocks:

Double Nine Patch block: 9" x 9"

Square-in-a-Square block: 2" x 2"

Materials

Yardages are based on 42"-wide fabric.

15 assorted dark 3"-wide strips for Nine Patch blocks and flying-geese units

10 assorted light 5"-wide strips for Nine Patch blocks and flying-geese units

36 assorted tan 3½" squares* for Double Nine Patch blocks

16 assorted red 2½" squares* for Square-in-a-Square blocks

¼ yard of medium-value checked fabric for Square-in-a-Square blocks

⅓ yard of dark blue print for binding

1¼ yards of fabric for backing

39" x 39" piece of batting

You can use charm squares trimmed to size, or cut squares from assorted strips or scraps.

Cutting

Measurements include ¼"-wide seam allowances.

From the assorted dark fabrics, cut:

216 rectangles, 1½" x 2½"

45 sets of 5 matching squares, 1½" x 1½" (225 total)

From the assorted light fabrics, cut:

45 sets of 4 matching squares, 1½" x 1½" (180 total)

216 pairs of matching connector squares, 1½" x 1½" (432 total)

From the medium-value checked fabric, cut:

64 connector squares, 1½" x 1½"

From the dark blue print, cut:

4 strips, 2¼" x 42"

Making the Double Nine Patch Blocks

Use four matching light 1½" squares and five matching dark 1½" squares for each block.

1 Sew the squares together in rows, pressing the seam allowances toward the darker fabrics. Then sew the rows together to make an individual Nine Patch block. Press the seam allowances in one direction. The block should measure 3½" x 3½". Make 45 Nine Patch blocks.

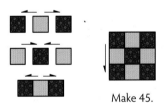

Make 45.

2 Randomly select five Nine Patch blocks and four assorted tan 3½" squares, and arrange them in Nine Patch fashion, starting with a Nine Patch block in the top-left corner and alternating them with the tan squares. Sew the pieced units and plain squares together in rows, pressing the seam allowances toward the tan squares. Then sew the rows together to complete a Double Nine Patch

block. Press. The block should measure 9½" x 9½". Press. Make nine Double Nine Patch blocks.

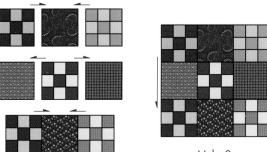

Make 9.

Making the Flying-Geese Sashing

1 Select a pair of matching light 1½" connector squares. Draw a diagonal line on the wrong side of each of these squares. Place a marked square on the short end of a dark 1½" x 2½" rectangle, right sides together. Sew on the drawn line. Trim the outside corner *of the connector square only,* ¼" from the stitching line. Press the seam allowances toward the corner. Repeat on the other end of the rectangle to complete one flying-geese unit. It should measure 1½" x 2½". Make 216 flying-geese units.

Make 216.

2 Randomly select nine flying-geese units and sew them together along their long edges to make a sashing strip. Make sure all of the dark triangles point in the same direction. Press the seam allowances toward the long edges of the dark triangles. The sashing strip should measure 2½" x 9½". Make 24 flying-geese sashing units.

Make 24.

Making the Square-in-a-Square Blocks

Sew four checked 1½" connector squares to a red 2½" square using the connecting square method described in step 1 of "Making the Flying-Geese Sashing" above.

Press the seam allowances toward the corners. The block should measure 2½" x 2½". Make 16 blocks.

Make 16.

Assembling and Finishing the Quilt

1 Arrange the Double Nine Patch blocks on a design wall or the floor, leaving 2½" between the blocks. Place a flying-geese sashing unit on each side of the block, taking care to orient the points in the proper direction. In the quilt shown, all dark triangles point toward the right across the top of the quilt, and then they alternate directions in each horizontal row. On the left edge of the quilt, the triangles point upward, in the next row downward, and so on. Finally, position the Square-in-a-Square blocks in the spaces between the sashing strips.

2 Once you are satisfied with the color placement, sew blocks and sashing pieces together in rows. Press the seam allowances toward the Nine Patch blocks. Join the rows to complete the quilt top. Press.

Quilt plan

3 Layer the backing, batting, and quilt top. Baste, and then quilt as desired.

4 Attach the dark blue 2¼"-wide binding strips.

Fruit Pie

One hundred Fruit Pie blocks are deliciously featured in a straight row setting, while their design adds diagonal movement. This block goes by many other names, including Double Hourglass, Attic Window, and Contrary Wife. Yet, none sound quite as sweet as Fruit Pie, cooling on a windowsill, made in anticipation of a loved one's return from war.

Quilt size: 30½" x 30½"
Finished block: 3" x 3"

Materials

Yardage is based on 42"-wide fabric.
¼ yard *each* of 12 assorted red prints for blocks
¼ yard *each* of 12 assorted blue prints for blocks
¼ yard *total* of assorted white prints for blocks
¼ yard of dark blue print for binding
1 yards of fabric for backing
34" x 34" piece of batting

Cutting

Measurements include ¼"-wide seam allowances.
From the assorted white prints, cut:
88 squares, 1⅞" x 1⅞"; cut squares in half diagonally
   to yield 176 triangles

From the assorted blue prints, cut:
180 squares, 1½" x 1½"
60 squares, 2⅞" x 2⅞"; cut squares in half diagonally
   to yield 120 triangles

From the assorted red prints, cut:
120 squares, 1½" x 1½"
40 squares, 2⅞" x 2⅞"; cut squares in half diagonally
   to yield 80 triangles
112 squares, 1⅞" x 1⅞"; cut squares in half diagonally
   to yield 224 triangles

From the dark blue print, cut:
4 strips, 2¼" x 42"

Making the Fruit Pie Blocks

All 100 blocks in this quilt are assembled the same way; only the color placement changes. You'll need four blue-and-muslin blocks for the quilt center, 40 red-and-muslin blocks for the second and fourth rounds, and 56 blue-and-red blocks for the remainder of the quilt.

Blue-and-White Blocks

1 Sew a white 1⅞" triangle to the right edge of a blue 1½" square. Make two matching. Press the seam allowances toward the blue squares.

Make 2.

2 Sew white 1⅞" triangles to opposite sides of a matching blue 1½" square. The bias side of one triangle (the long diagonal edge) should be facing up and the bias side of the second triangle should be facing down as shown. Press the seam allowances toward the blue square.

Make 1.

3 Sew the units from step 1 to the top and bottom of the unit from step 2, matching seam intersections. Press the seam allowances toward the outer edges of the unit.

4 Sew a matching blue 2⅞" triangle to each side of the above unit. Be careful not to stretch the bias edges when stitching and pressing. The block should measure 3½" x 3½". Make four blue-and-white blocks.

Make 4.

Red-and-White Blocks

These blocks are made exactly like the blue-and-white blocks, except you'll replace the blue triangles and squares with red ones. Make 40 red-and-white blocks.

Make 40.

Blue-and-Red Blocks

Again, these blocks are made in the same manner as the other blocks. For each block, you'll use three blue 1½" squares, two blue 2⅞" triangles, and four red 1⅞" triangles. Make 56 blue-and-red blocks.

Make 56.

Assembling and Finishing the Quilt

1 Following the quilt plan for color placement and block orientation, arrange the blocks into 10 rows of 10 blocks each.

2 Sew the blocks together in rows, pressing the seam allowances in opposite directions from row to row. Then join the rows, matching points carefully. Press.

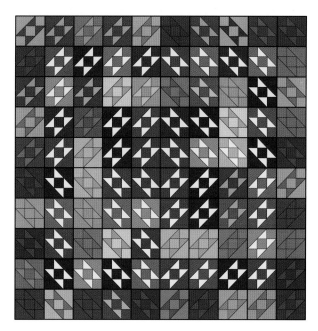

Quilt plan

3 Layer the backing, batting, and quilt top. Baste, and then quilt as desired.

4 Attach the blue 2¼"-wide binding strips.

This lap-sized quilt is just the place to display your patriotic colors. Combine red, blue, gray, and cream prints, for a scrappy blend of easy Four Patch blocks and appliquéd stars.

Quilt size: 41½" x 65½"
Finished blocks: Star block: 12" x 12"
Four Patch block: 12" x 12"

Materials

Yardage is based on 42"-wide fabric, unless otherwise noted. Fat quarters are approximately 18" x 21".

¼ yard *each* of 8 light prints for background of Star blocks and sashing on Four Patch blocks

¼ yard *each* of 8 red prints for star appliqués and Four Patch blocks

⅛ yard *each* of 8 dark blue prints for Star blocks and Four Patch blocks

8 fat quarters of medium blue prints for circle appliqués

⅜ yard of blue-gray checked fabric for border

⅝ yard of blue plaid for binding

2¾ yards of fabric for backing (pieced horizontally)

45" x 69" piece of batting

Template plastic

Optional: freezer paper or fusible web

Cutting

Measurements include ¼"-wide seam allowances. Make templates of the star and circle patterns (page 71) and prepare star shape for hand or fusible appliqué.

From *each* of the red prints, cut:
2 squares, 4¼" x 4¼" (16 total; you will have 2 left over)
6 squares, 3" x 3" (48 total)
1 star (8 total)

From *each* of the medium blue prints, cut:
1 square, 8" x 8" (8 total)

From *each* of the light prints, cut:
1 square, 8" x 8" (8 total)
6 squares, 3⅜" x 3⅜"; cut squares in half diagonally to yield 12 triangles (96 total)
3 squares, 3" x 3" (24 total)
4 rectangles, 3" x 8" (32 total; you will have 4 left over)

From *each* of the dark blue prints, cut:
2 squares, 4¼" x 4¼" (16 total; you will have 2 left over)
6 squares, 3⅜" x 3⅜"; cut squares in half diagonally to yield 12 triangles (96 total)
3 squares, 3" x 3" (24 total)

From the blue-gray checked fabric, cut:
4 strips, 3" x 42"; crosscut into 16 rectangles, 3" x 8"

From the blue plaid, cut:
2¼"-wide bias strips, enough to yield 224" of binding

Making the Star Blocks

For more information on appliqué techniques, visit ShopMartingale.com/HowtoQuilt for free downloadable instructions.

1 Using your favorite appliqué method, appliqué a star to a medium blue 8" square. When the star is complete, position the circle template over the star, making sure each point of the star is touching the circle edge. Mark and cut out the circle, leaving a narrow turn-under allowance. (Or, if you're using fusible web, cut out the circle on the line *after* you've applied fusible web to the wrong side of the fabric.) Appliqué the circle/star unit to a light 8" square.

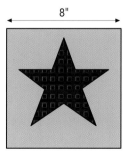

Appliqué star to square.   Mark circle.

2 Using 12 light triangles that match the star background from step 1 and a set of 12 matching dark blue triangles, sew the triangles together to make 12 half-square-triangle units. Press the seam allowances toward the blue triangles. Sew the half-square-triangle units together in rows of three as shown. Make four rows. Press the seam allowances toward the blue triangles.

Make 12 matching.

Make 4 rows.

3 Sew rows of triangles to opposite sides of the appliqué block, with the light triangles adjoining the block. Press the seam allowances toward the appliqué block.

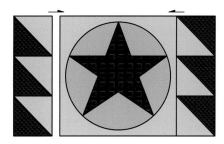

4 On the remaining two triangle rows, sew a red 3" square to the light end of the row and a light 3" square to the blue end of the row. Press the seam allowances toward the squares. Sew these strips to the top and bottom of the unit from step 3; press the seam allowances away from the center unit. The block should measure 12½" x 12½". Make eight blocks.

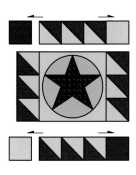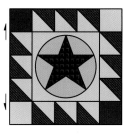

Make 8.

Making the Four Patch Blocks

1 Using two matching red 4½" squares and two matching dark blue 4½" squares, sew the squares together to make a four-patch unit as shown. Press the seam allowances as indicated.

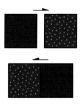

2 Select four matching light 3" x 8" rectangles. Sew one to the left side and one to the right side of the four-patch unit. To the remaining two rectangles, sew a red 3" square to one end and a dark blue 3" square to the other end; make two matching. Press all seam allowances toward the rectangles. Sew these units to the top and bottom of the four-patch unit. Press all seam allowances toward the rectangles. The block should measure 12½" x 12½". Make seven Four Patch blocks.

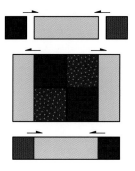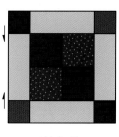

Make 7.

Making the Border Units

Sew a red 3" square to a blue-gray 3" x 8" rectangle. Make 16 units. Sew a dark blue 3" square to the opposite end of 10 of the rectangles. Sew a light 3" square to the opposite end of the remaining six units.

Make 10.   Make 6.

Assembling the Quilt

1 Arrange the blocks in five rows of three blocks each, alternating the Star blocks with the Four Patch blocks. Position the border units at the end of each row, taking care to position the red, blue, or light squares according to the quilt assembly diagram.

2 For the top and bottom rows, arrange the remaining border units, referring to the diagram. Place a red 3" square in the top-left and bottom-right corners; position a light 3" square in the two remaining corners.

3 When you're pleased with the arrangement, sew the rows together; press the seam allowances toward the Four Patch blocks. Join the rows. Press the seam allowances in one direction.

4 Layer the backing, batting, and quilt top. Baste, and then quilt as desired.

5 Attach the blue plaid 2¼"-wide binding strips.

Quilt assembly

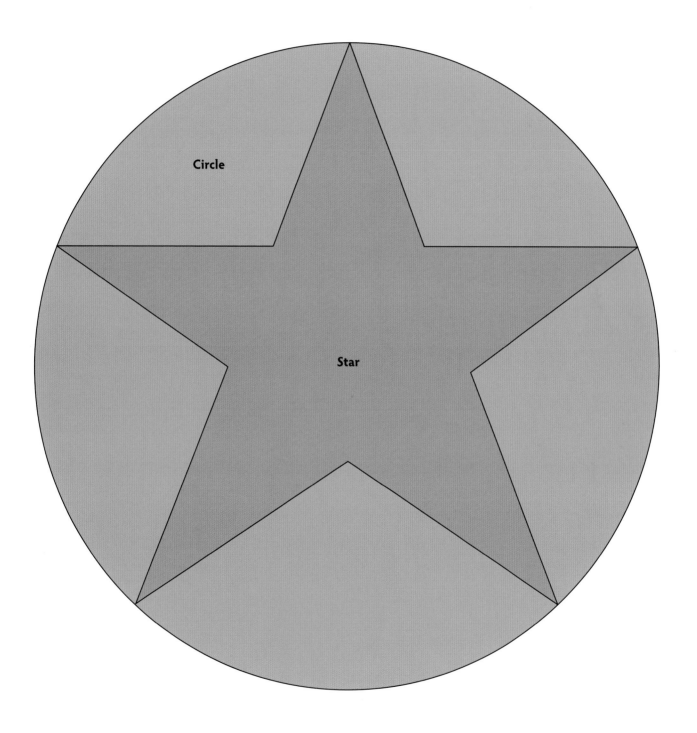

Circle

Star

I magine time ticking away, hours, days, weeks, months, as a loved one was far away on a battlefield, with no word—no email, phone calls, or instant messages. In today's modern world, you can while away the hours in style with a scrappy table runner made of easy Hourglass blocks.

Quilt size: 22½" x 46½"
Finished block: 4" x 4"

Materials

Yardages are based on 42"-wide fabric. Fat eigths are approximately 9" x 21".
6 fat eighths of dark red, brown, and gold prints for blocks
6 fat eighths of light and medium tan prints for blocks
⅓ yard of medium tan striped (running crosswise) fabric for border
¼ yard of medium pink print for border
⅓ yard of brown print for binding
1½ yards of fabric for backing
26" x 50" piece of batting

Cutting

Measurements include ¼"-wide seam allowances.
From the dark prints, cut:
20 squares, 5¼" x 5¼"; cut squares into quarters diagonally to yield 80 triangles

From the light and medium tan prints, cut:
20 squares, 5¼" x 5¼"; cut squares into quarters diagonally to yield 80 triangles

From the medium tan striped fabric, cut:*
2 strips, 3½" x 32½"
2 rectangles, 3½" x 8½"

*We chose to fussy cut the striped fabric for our border. If you choose this type of look, you might need to change the width of your border pieces to accommodate the stripe in the fabric.

From the medium pink print, cut:
4 rectangles, 3½" x 7½"
4 rectangles, 3½" x 4½"

From the brown print, cut:
4 strips, 2¼" x 42"

Making the Hourglass Blocks

Use one light (or medium) and one dark print for each block. Join two dark triangles and two medium or light triangles to make an Hourglass block. Press the seam allowances as indicated. The block should measure 4½" x 4½". Make 40 blocks.

Make 40.

Assembling and Finishing the Quilt

1 Arrange the Hourglass blocks in 10 rows of four blocks each, rotating the blocks so that the lights and darks alternate from block to block. Sew the blocks together in rows, pressing the seam allowances in opposite directions from row to row. Join the rows. Press the seam allowances in one direction.

Quilt assembly

2 Sew a tan striped 3½" x 8½" rectangle between two pink 3½" x 7½" rectangles. Press the seam allowances toward the pink rectangles. Make two borders for the top and bottom of the quilt. Sew a pink 3½" x 4½" rectangle to each end of a tan striped

3½" x 32½" strip. Press the seam allowances toward the pink rectangles. Make two side borders.

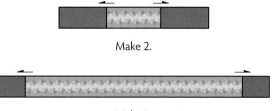

Make 2.

Make 2.

3 Sew the top and bottom borders to the quilt top. Press the seam allowances toward the borders. Sew the side borders to the quilt top. Press the seam allowances toward the borders.

Quilt plan

4 Layer the backing, batting, and quilt top. Baste, and then quilt as desired.

5 Attach the brown 2¼"-wide binding strips.

This pair of doll-sized quilts is perfect for any little girl or for anyone else who collects dolls. These quilts would look terrific displayed with a vintage doll or two. They're both reminiscent of make-do quilts that were commonly sewn to use up every bit of leftover fabric, whether from other quilts or clothing, and to teach young girls how to sew.

On-Point Four Patch

Quilt size: 16⅜" x 26"

Materials

⅛ yard *each* of 2 dark brown prints for four-patch units
¼ yard of pink print for triangles
¼ yard of dark brown striped fabric for rows
¼ yard of medium brown geometric print for triangles
¼ yard of light brown striped fabric for triangles
¼ yard of pink-and-brown striped fabric for rows
¼ yard of brown print for outer rows
¼ yard of dark brown print for binding
⅝ yard of fabric for backing
21" x 30" piece of batting

Cutting

Measurements include ¼"-wide seam allowances.
From *each* of the 2 dark brown prints, cut:
1 strip, 1½" x 42"; crosscut into 18 squares, 1½" x 1½" (36 total)

From the pink print, cut:
4 squares, 4½" x 4½"; cut squares into quarters diagonally to yield 16 triangles
2 squares, 2¾" x 2¾"; cut squares in half diagonally to yield 4 triangles

From the dark brown striped fabric, cut:
2 strips, 2" x 42"

From *each* of the medium brown geometric print and light brown striped fabric, cut:
4 squares, 5¼" x 5¼"; cut squares into quarters diagonally to yield 16 triangles. You will have 2 left over.

From the pink-and-brown striped fabric, cut:
2 strips, 2" x 42"

From the brown print for outer rows, cut:
2 strips, 2" x 42"

From the dark brown print for binding, cut:
3 strips, 2¼" x 42"

Making the Quilt

1 Sew two 1½" squares from each of the dark brown prints together to form a four-patch unit. The unit should measure 2½" x 2½". Make nine.

Make 9.

2 Sew two 4½" pink triangles to opposite sides of a four-patch unit to create a diagonal row as shown. Make seven. Sew these units together. Press.

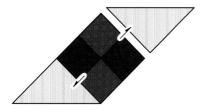

Make 7.

Lop off Row Ends for an Antique Look
The triangle rows made in step 5 will be too long for your quilt top. And that's just what we wanted! You can center the rows on each side of the quilt top and then cut off the excess. It won't be exact and the triangle points at the end of each row most likely will be cut off and no longer pointy. But that's part of what gives this little quilt the charm of an antique quilt. Doll quilts made by young girls or even their mothers weren't made with the precision of a rotary cutter and ruler that measured in exact ⅛" increments!

3 Make two end units for the Four Patch row as shown, using one pink 4½" triangle and two pink 2¾" triangles for each. Join these units to the row from step 2.

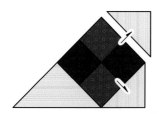

Make 2.

Make 1 row.

4 Sew a dark brown striped strip to each side of the Four Patch row. Let the strip extend at either end for later trimming.

5 Sew the brown geometric print triangles together with the light brown striped triangles, alternating them as shown. You'll need seven triangles of each color per row. Make two rows. Press. Sew the triangle strips to the brown striped rows with the light brown strip adjoining the dark brown rows.

Make 2 rows.

6 Center and sew a pink-and-brown striped strip and a brown print strip to each side of the quilt. Press all seam allowances outward.

7 Square up the quilt top, trimming off the ragged ends of the rows along the top and bottom of the quilt, regardless of where the triangles lie.

Quilt plan

8 Layer the backing, batting, and quilt top. Baste, and then quilt as desired.

9 Attach the dark brown 2¼"-wide binding strips.

Checkerboard Strippy Quilt

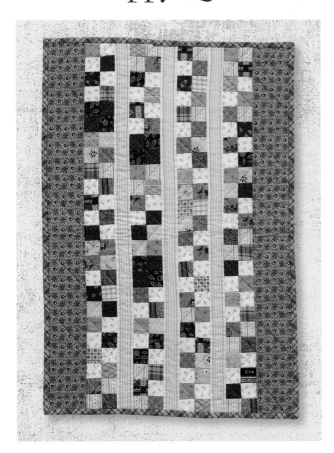

Quilt size: 16½" x 24½"

Materials

¼ yard *each* of 10 assorted light, pink, and brown
   fabrics for checkerboard rows*
¼ yard of pink striped fabric for rows
¼ yard of brown print for rows
Fat quarter of brown plaid for bias binding
⅝ yard of fabric for backing
20" x 28" piece of batting
* If you are using scraps you will need ⅓ yard total fabric.

Cutting

Measurements include ¼"-wide seam allowances.
From the assorted light, pink, and brown fabrics, cut:
192 squares, 1½" x 1½"

From the pink striped fabric, cut:
3 strips, 1½" x 25"

From the brown print, cut:
2 strips, 3" x 42"

From the brown plaid, cut:
2¼"-wide bias strips, enough to yield 90" of binding

Making the Quilt

1 Sew the 1½" squares together in random pairs.
   Sew 24 pairs together to make a row. Make four
   checkerboard rows.

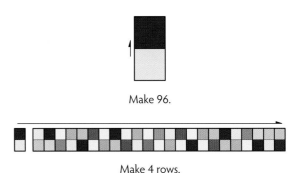

Make 96.

Make 4 rows.

2 Trim each of the pink striped strips to 24½" long.
   Sew the pink strips between the checkerboard
   rows according to the quilt plan. Trim the brown
   print strips to 24½" long and sew one to each outer
   edge of the quilt top. Press all strips away from the
   checkerboard strips.

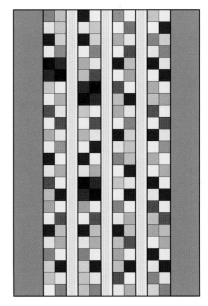

Quilt plan

3 Layer the backing, batting, and quilt top. Baste, and
   then quilt as desired.
4 Attach the brown plaid 2¼"-wide bias-binding strips.

About the Authors

Mary and Janey; photo by Susan Henderson

Connie and Lucy; photo by Roy Tesene

I've lived on the Country Threads farm for 34 years and love my life in the country! I also love animals and am active in dog transport and rescue. I drive my "leg" of a transport many Saturdays or Sundays, meeting the previous driver who brings the dogs to a meeting place near my home. We transfer the dogs to my van and I drive them north about 70 miles to another parking lot, where someone meets me and takes the dogs to the Minneapolis area. There the dogs live in foster homes belonging to members of the rescue groups who have arranged to have them pulled from kill shelters in the south. The search then begins to find each dog a forever home.

I have four rescued dogs: Izzy, a golden doodle; Maggie, a golden retriever; Janey, a Jack Russell terrier; and Benjie, a schnauzer mix. My next endeavor will be a cage-free dog-boarding business on the Country Threads farm.

I live just three miles from Mary's farm in Garner with my husband, Roy; two cats; and Lucy, our yellow Lab. We raised our three boys in this town of 3000 people, and now our kids and grandkids come for visits and are amazed at the freedoms small-town life can bring. I've always loved to garden, and several years ago I participated in the Master Gardener program. Our 100-year-old home is surrounded by huge shade trees, so I've planted dozens and dozens of hosta varieties. I still sew every day and love it. My sewing room is located above our three-stall garage and is full of fabric in old cupboards. We are blessed at Country Threads not only with wonderful fabric, but with great friends, customers, employees, animals, and plants.

About Country Threads

Country Threads is located on a farm in northern Iowa.

Connie Tesene and Mary Etherington have been business partners at Country Threads since 1983, shortly after both moved to Garner, Iowa. The business started as a wholesale quilt-pattern company that soon expanded into a retail quilt shop on Mary's small farm in north-central Iowa. Today the farm is home to the quilt shop, the wholesale operation, the machine-quilting business, and numerous farm animals, many of whom will greet you when you arrive. Camp is held several times a year in the haymow of the barn, where friends from across the nation gather to sew together for four days.

Connie and Mary have published over 800 individual patterns and more than 20 quilt-pattern books. Even though the business has expanded over the past 30 years, the farm is still home to fancy chickens, geese, goats, dogs, and cats. Visitors enjoy the interaction with the cats in the quilt shop and come to know the pets on a personal basis through the Goat Gazette newsletter and the free email newsletter. Find out more online at CountyThreads.com.

Country Threads' mission statement: where no goat has ever been denied, where no cat has ever been disciplined, and where no dog has ever been discouraged . . . and where quilting is alive and well!